D1708928

This Workbook Belongs to:

●●●●●●●●●●●●●●

How to use this workbook:

Affirmations can be very powerful!
Especially for young children.
Children absorb so much!
In the early years of development, they are
learning how the world works and who they
are.
Give them the foundation of healthy and
positive words that affirm who they are.
It will help them build a foundation of
empowerment and confidence and develop a
growth mindset that will make a lasting impact.

Have the child trace the affirmation and
when they are finished, have them repeat it
out loud.

We hope you enjoy this workbook and see your
child's handwriting skills imporve and their sense
of self soar!

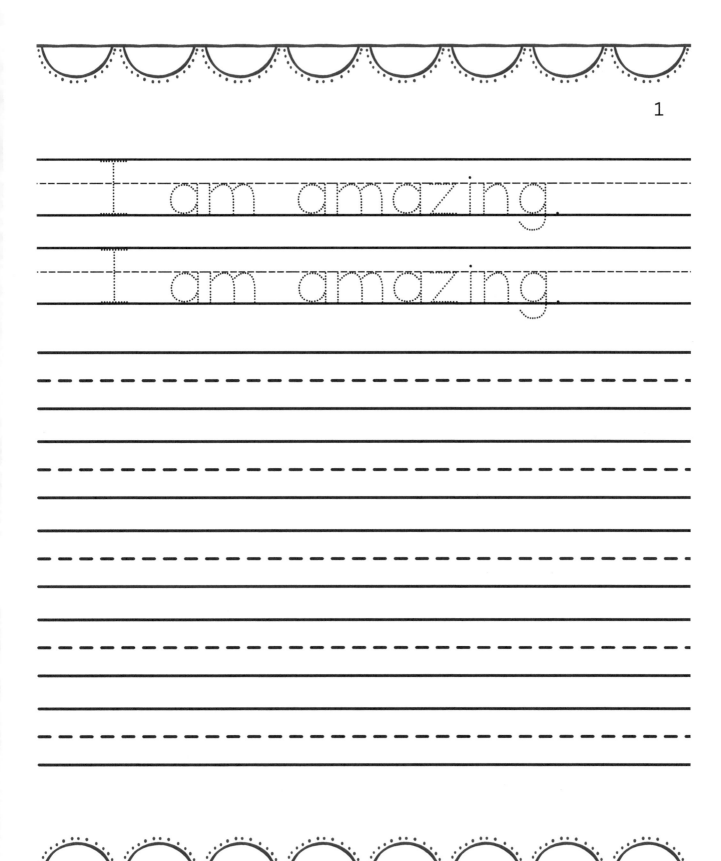

I am amazing.

I am amazing.

I am strong.

I am strong.

I am brave.

I am brave.

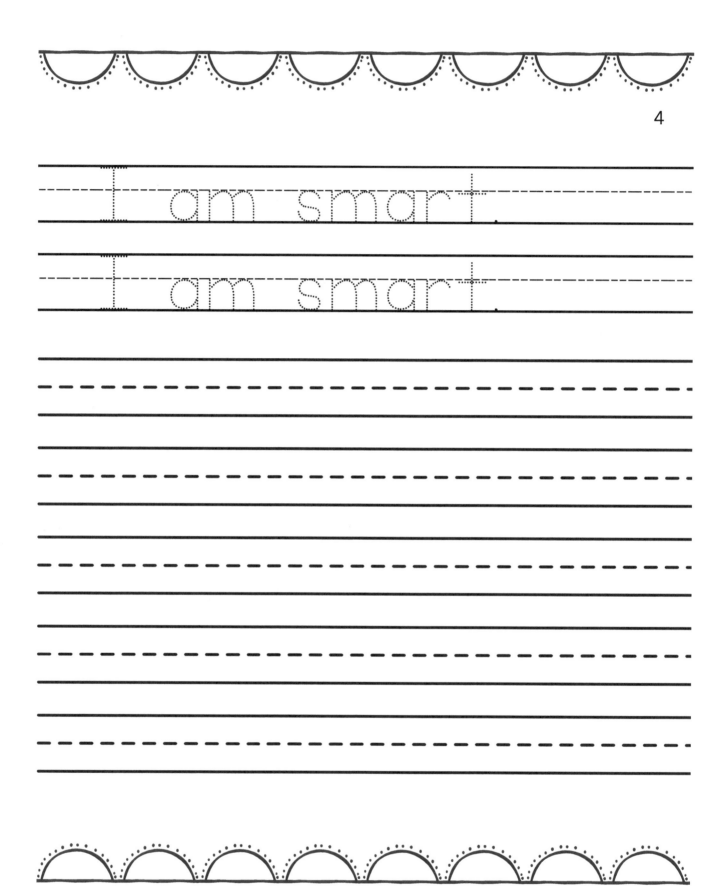

I am smart.

I am smart.

I am helpful.

I am helpful.

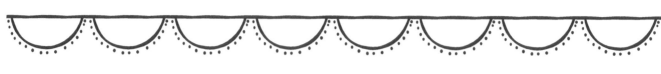

I am grateful.

I am grateful.

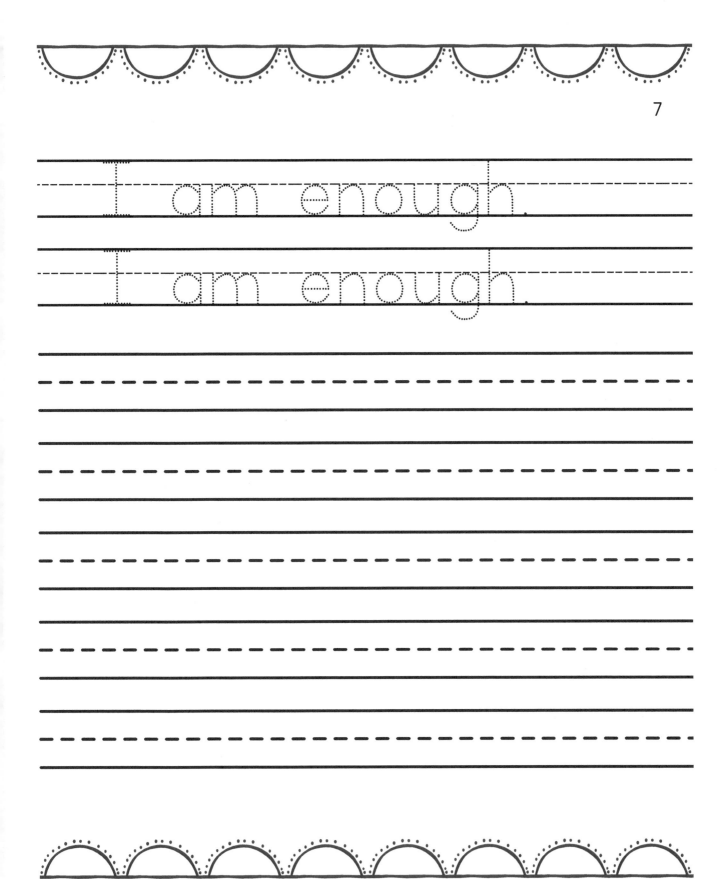

7

I am enough.

I am enough.

I am unique.

I am unique.

I am loved.

I am loved.

I am respectful.

I am respectful.

I am confident.

I am confident.

I can do this.

I can do this.

I am important.

I am important.

I love learning.

I love learning.

I matter.

I matter.

I am special.

I am special.

I am responsible.

I am responsible.

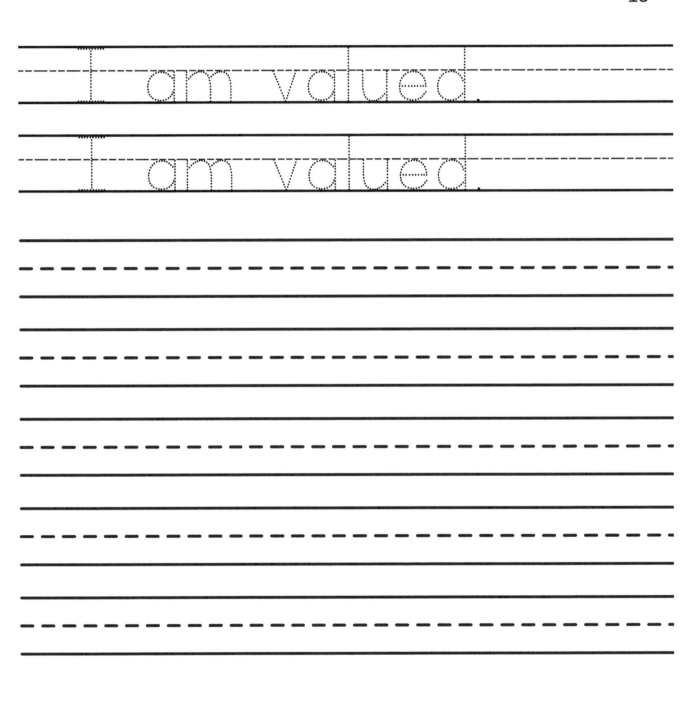

I am valued.

I am valued.

I am talented.

I am talented.

I love myself.

I love myself.

I love others.

I love others.

My voice matters.

My voice matters.

23

I am resilient.

I am resilient.

I am successful.

I am successful.

I am powerful.

I am powerful.

I work hard.

I work hard.

My best
is enough.

I can ask.

for help.

My mistakes help me grow.

I can do
hard things.

I have people.
who love me.

Progress, not
perfection.

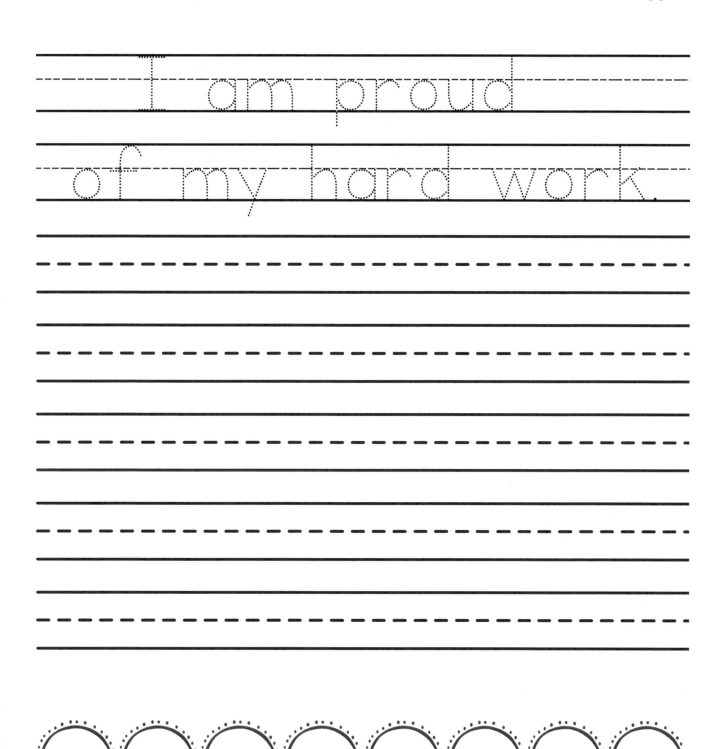

33

I am proud
of my hard work.

I get better
every single day.

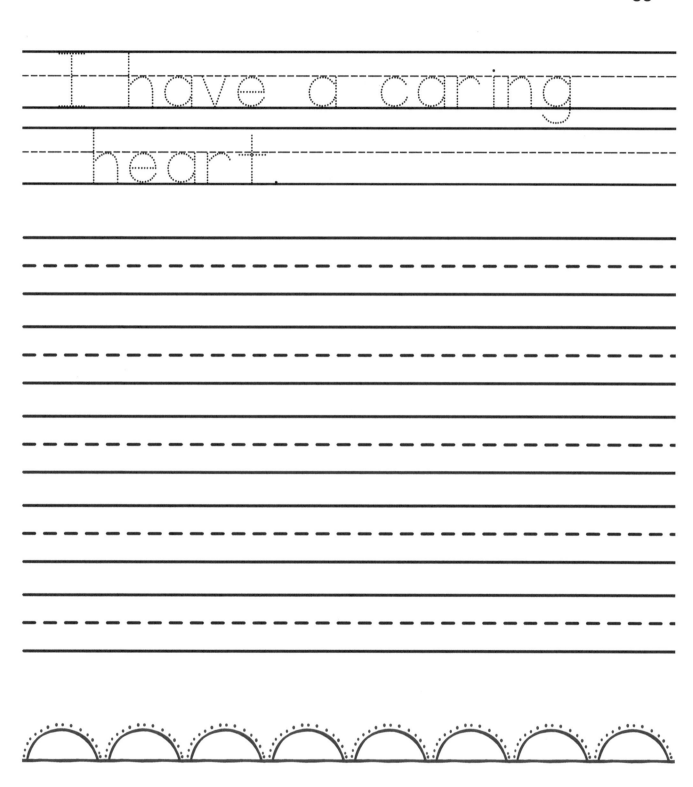

35

I have a caring
heart.

I am playful, fun, and creative.

I love to learn new things.

I am wonderful
just as I am.

Today, I will shine.

My future is bright.

I can ask for a
hug when I'm sad.

45

47

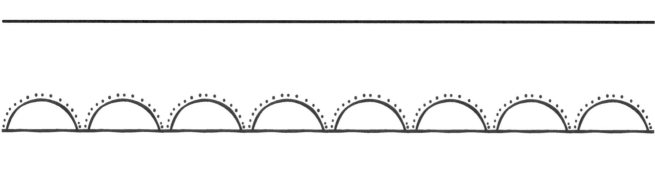

Made in United States
Troutdale, OR
06/05/2023

10453156R00037